Seasons Around You

Summer

Saviour Pirotta

WAYLAND

Seasons Around You

 Autumn

 Spring

Summer

Winter

Cover photograph: Fun in the swimming pool.

Title page: Milkshakes are a favourite summer drink.

Produced for Wayland Publishers Ltd by
Roger Coote Publishing
Gissing's Farm, Fressingfield
Eye, Suffolk IP21 5SH, England

Series designer: Jan Stirling
Book designer: Victoria Webb

First published in 1998 by
Wayland Publishers Limited
61 Western Road, Hove
East Sussex BN3 1JD, England

Find Wayland on the Internet at http://www.wayland.co.uk

British Library Cataloguing in Publication Data
Pirotta, Saviour, 1958–
    Summer. – (Seasons around you)
    1. Summer – Pictorial works – Juvenile literature
    I. Title
    508.2

    ISBN 0 7502 2276 X

Printed and bound in Italy by EuroGrafica, Vicenza.

Picture acknowledgements
Angela Hampton Family Life Pictures 12, 13, 15, 16;
Frank Lane Picture Agency 10 (Bringard/Sunset), 18
(STF/Sunset), 21 (STF/Sunset), 22 (Tony Hamblin), 23 (J
Watkins), 25 (G E Hyde); Getty Images *front cover* (Peter
Correz), 5 (John Chard), 6 (Charles Thatcher), 7 (Dennis
O'Clair), 8 (Joe McBride), 9 (Alan Hicks), 17 (Martin
Chaffer), 19 (Peter Correz), 26–27 (Suzanne and Nick
Geary), 28 (Doug Armand); Robert Harding Picture
Library 14 (A Des Essartons), 27 (M H Black); Tim
Woodcock Photography 1, 11, 20, 24, 29 (Harry Graham);
Zefa 4.

Contents

Words that appear in **bold** are explained in the glossary on page 32.

Summer is here

Summer brings bright, sunny days.
The skies are blue, the air is warm and
the days are long.

Sometimes it gets so hot that
there is a **thunderstorm**.
A rainbow forms in the sky.

Cool summer clothes

In summer we wear light, thin clothes that keep us cool – shorts, T-shirts and summery dresses.

Sunglasses protect our eyes from the bright sun. They are fun to wear, too.

Sun protection

When we stay out in the sun, we put on **sun-tan lotion**. It protects our skin from the sun's harmful rays.

We wear sunhats, too. They keep
the sun off our heads
and faces.

Summer at school

At school, sometimes we have
lessons outside on the grass.
If we're lucky, we might go on a trip, too.

There is the school **fête** and sports day.
Then we break up for the long
summer holidays.

Holiday time

Many people go on holiday in the summer.
Some families go camping.

Some people go to the seaside.
It's great fun going to the beach.
We can splash in the sea for hours.

Day trips and picnics

Sometimes we go for a day out in the countryside. It's fun having picnics outdoors.

It's fun to visit the zoo, too. We learn
a lot about animals and buy sweets and
souvenirs from the gift shop.

Summer food

In summer we eat cold foods like salads and fruits. Sometimes we have ice-cream.

Some people have **barbecues**.
The smell of the food cooking
makes everyone feel hungry!

Fun and games

It's fun to play outdoors in the summer.
Sometimes we ride our bikes or fly kites.

It's warm enough to go swimming in outdoor swimming pools. We put on our swimming costumes and jump in.

Water, water!

It's easy to get thirsty in the summer.
We have cold drinks like milkshakes.

The plants in the garden need lots of water. We have to water them every day.

Birds in summer

On warm, sunny days, birds stretch out their wings and sunbathe.

Birds are always looking for water.
They drink and bathe in birdbaths
or ponds.

Hungry insects

In fields and gardens, caterpillars munch their way through juicy, green leaves.

Wasps eat into the summer fruits.
Bumblebees collect sweet **nectar**
from the flowers.

25

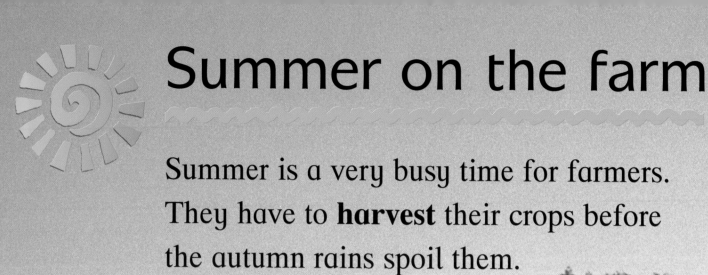

Summer on the farm

Summer is a very busy time for farmers. They have to **harvest** their crops before the autumn rains spoil them.

Pigs get very hot.
They roll around in
the mud to keep cool.

Festivals and fairs

Summer is the time for festivals and fairs.
Sometimes there are parades with **floats**.
People dress up and dance in the street.

There is lots to do at fairgrounds. We might have our faces painted. We can play on the bouncy castle or go on a fairground ride.

Summer activities

 SCIENCE

Light and sound Make a list of all the sounds you can hear by the sea, like the lapping of the waves, the music of the ice-cream van and the shouting of children. Now get members of your class to recreate the sounds and record them all on tape. You could use this as background for a play or mime show.

Summer is the season of light. Find some of the many legends about the sun and retell one of them in a comic book. Why do you think that the sun is so important to so many people? What would happen if there were no sun? What effect would it have on the environment and us?

Humans as organisms Many different types of fruit and vegetables grow in the summer. Find out what fresh foods are available in summer and why they are good for you. Draw up a fact sheet about good food and distribute it to the rest of the school.

Living things in the environment Look at the plants and trees in your wildlife area or local park and make a list of them. You could also take pictures of them. Compare them with plants you can see in books on the rain forest. Are all the plants different? Are there any that grow in both environments? What do you think would happen if you grew rain forest plants in your local park? Would any of them survive?

 HISTORY

Chronology Using the books in your school or public library, find out what bathing costumes and sunglasses looked like in the past. Draw pictures of your friends wearing some of the costumes. Would they find them comfortable to wear?

 GEOGRAPHY

Comparing localities Summer is ideal for playing outdoor games. Look in books in your library and find games played by children in other countries. Are any of the games similar to the games you play?

Have you been on holiday this year? Draw a picture of your holiday, perhaps showing the place you stayed in, where you played and the food you ate. Ask your friends to draw pictures of their holidays, too. Then talk about the differences between them. Was the food you ate the same as your friends? Who went to the hottest place? Who went to the coolest?

Find out what cold drinks people have in other countries. The list should include fizzy drinks, fruit and vegetable juices and different types of water and milk.

 DESIGN AND TECHNOLOGY

Design and make some cardboard frames for sunglasses. Use summer colours and patterns.

Design a theme park your friends might want to visit. Think of a local spot where you could build it and what local people might want to see and do there. Don't forget to include attractions, rides, refreshment areas, toilets and gift shops.

 DANCE AND DRAMA

Summer is the time when we think of the sea and faraway islands. Find a sea legend, perhaps involving mermaids or sunken treasure, and use it as the basis for a summer play. There are some exciting Caribbean stories you might want to find or, if you live close to the sea, you might want to adapt a local legend.

Topic web

DANCE AND DRAMA
Carnival
Music

SCIENCE
Plants and trees
Hot and cold habitats
Sea sounds
Sounds of the countryside
Light and dark
Humans as organisms
Healthy foods

GEOGRAPHY
Cold countries, hot countries
Environment: roads, forests, farms, cities
Comparing localities: holiday locations
Lands and buildings: farms, houses
Attractive and unattractive: improving environment
Local environment: park

SEASONS TOPIC WEB

HISTORY
Chronology
History of swimwear
History of sunglasses

DESIGN AND TECHNOLOGY
Sunhats
Sunglasses
Design a theme park

MATHS
Measuring and comparing hours of daylight
Sequence of seasons

Resources

NON-FICTION
Weather Facts by P. Eden and C. Twist (Dorling Kindersley, 1995)

Seasonal Crafts: Summer by Gillian Chapman (Wayland, 1997)

Clothes in Hot and Cold Places by Simon Crisp (Wayland, 1996)

Exploring Seaside Towns by Danielle Sensier and Amanda Earl (Wayland, 1997)

Get Set, Go… Summer by Ruth Thomson (Watts, 1997)

Summer on the Farm by Janet Fitzgerald (Evans, 1995)

Seashore Animals by Gwen Allen and Joan Denslow (OUP, 1997)

The Seasons by Debbie MacKinnon (Frances Lincoln, 1995)

FICTION AND POETRY
Summer Story by Jill Barklem (Collins Brambly Hedge series, 1980). The adventures of the mice of Brambly Hedge, with illustrations showing the countryside in summer.

Poems for Summer by Robert Hull (Wayland, 1995). Seasonal poems from around the world, illustrated with colour photographs.

Glossary

Barbecues Meals that are cooked outdoors over open fires.

Fête A fair, usually held outside.

Floats Large, flat trucks that carry people or displays in a festival parade. They are usually decorated with flowers, streamers or colourful scenes.

Harvest When farmers and gardeners gather their crops.

Nectar A sweet, sticky liquid that insects drink out of flowers.

Souvenirs Things that you buy to remind you of a holiday or a visit.

Sun-tan lotion Special cream that we put on to stop our skins being damaged or burned by the powerful rays of the sun.

Thunderstorm A storm caused by rising warm air. There is thunder, heavy rain and often there is lightning too.

Index